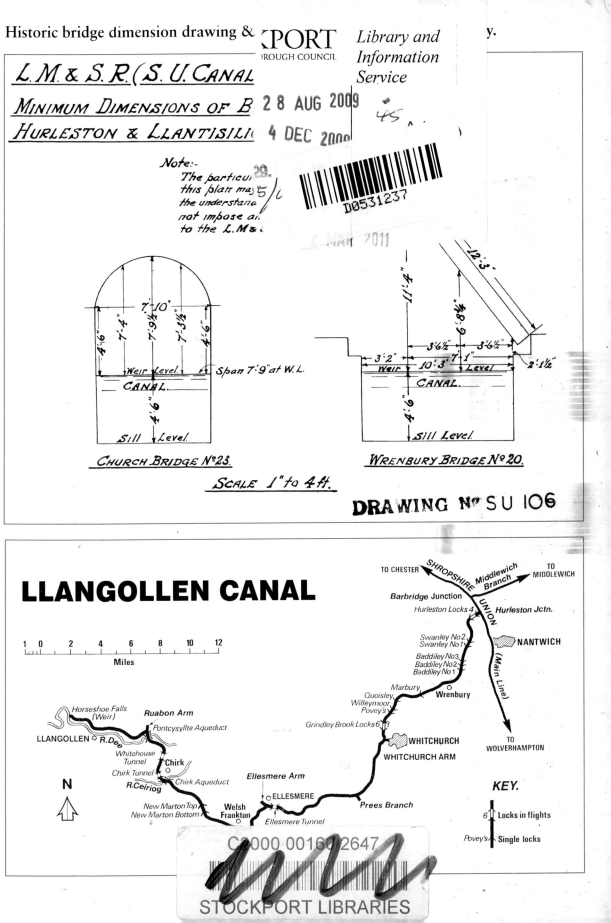

L. M. & S. R. (S. U. CANAL ...

MINIMUM DIMENSIONS OF B...

HURLESTON & LLANTISILI...

Note:-
The particul...
this plan ma...
the understan...
not impose a...
to the L. M & ...

CHURCH BRIDGE Nº 23.

7'·10"
7'·4"
7'·9¾"
7'·3½"
4'·6"
4'·6"

Weir Level.   Span 7'·9 at W.L.
CANAL.
4'·6"
Sill Level.

WRENBURY BRIDGE Nº 20.

12'·3"
11'·4"
6'·8¾"
3'·6½"   3'·6½"
3'·2"   7'·1"   2'·1½"
Weir   10'·3"   Level
CANAL.
4'·6"
Sill Level.

SCALE 1" to 4 ft.

DRAWING Nº SU 106

LLANGOLLEN CANAL

1 0   2   4   6   8   10   12
Miles

N

TO CHESTER   SHROPSHIRE   Middlewich   TO
Barbridge Junction   Branch   MIDDLEWICH
Hurleston Locks 4   Hurleston Jctn.
Swanley No 2
Swanley No 1   NANTWICH
Baddiley No 3
Baddiley No 2
Baddiley No 1   (Main Line)
Marbury
Quoisley   Wrenbury
Willeymoor
Povey's
Grindley Brook Locks 6
WHITCHURCH
WHITCHURCH ARM
TO
WOLVERHAMPTON
UNION

Horseshoe Falls (Weir)   Ruabon Arm
Pontcysyllte Aqueduct
LLANGOLLEN   R.Dee
Whitehouse Tunnel   Chirk
Chirk Tunnel   Chirk Aqueduct
R.Ceiriog
New Marton Top   Welsh   Ellesmere Arm
New Marton Bottom   Frankton   ELLESMERE   Prees Branch
Ellesmere Tunnel

KEY.

6 Locks in flights
Povey's Single locks

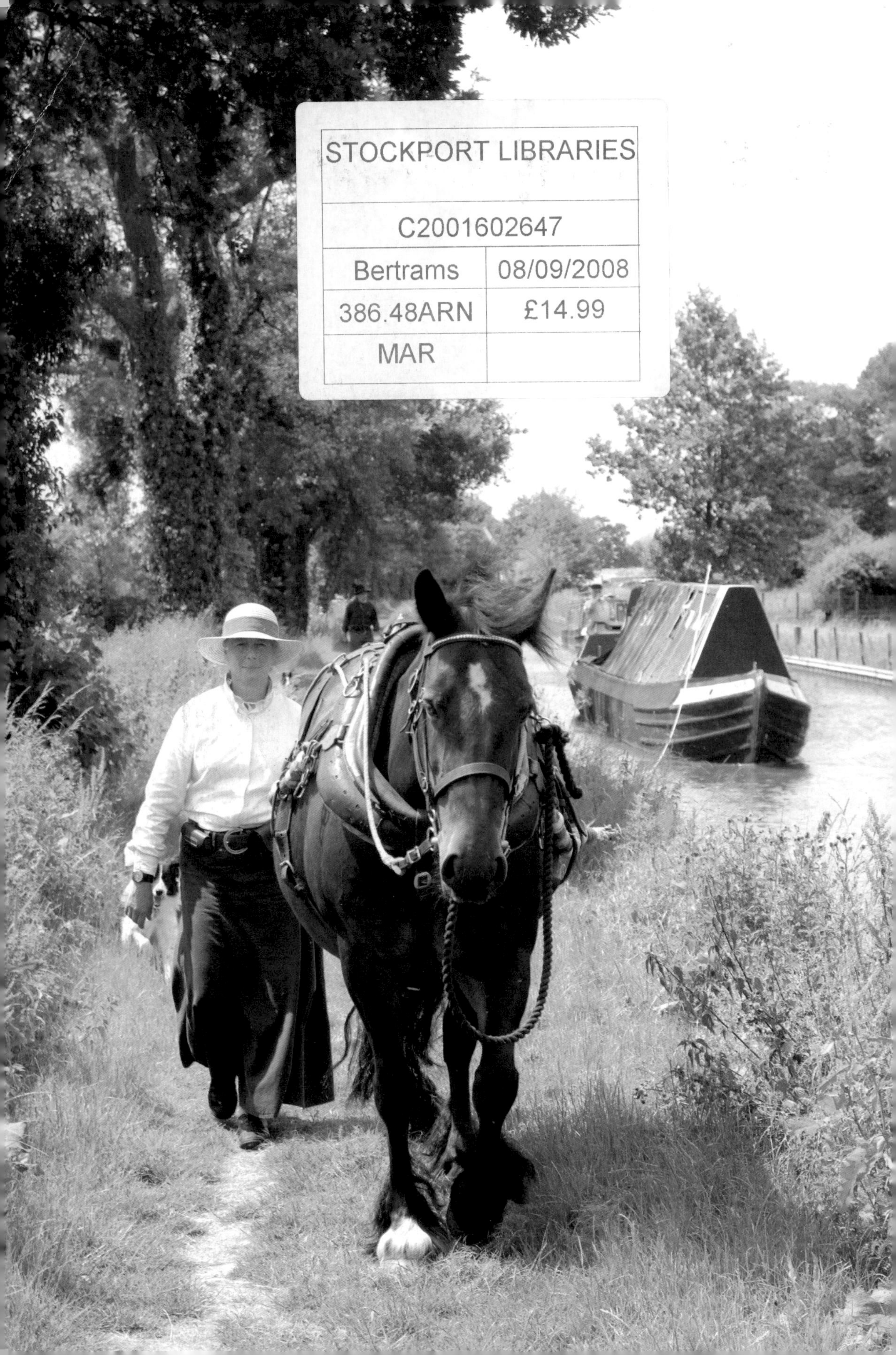

The Llangollen Canal

Harry Arnold

Dedicated to my wife Beryl, whose original idea it was to have a holiday on the Llangollen Canal, and our good friend Eddie, the third member of our then novice crew.

Landmark Publishing

Published by

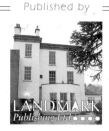

LANDMARK
Publishing Ltd

Ashbourne Hall, Cokayne Ave
Ashbourne, Derbyshire DE6 1EJ England
Tel: (01335) 347349 Fax: (01335) 347303
e-mail: landmark@clara.net
web site: www.landmarkpublishing.co.uk

ISBN 13: 978-1-84306-335-3

Printed by: Gutenberg Press, Malta

Designed by: Michelle Prost

Front Cover: The world famous Pontcysyllte Aqueduct

Back Cover Top: One of the canal's well-known features - the lift bridge

Back cover Bottom: Horseshoe Falls - where the River Dee feeds the canal

Back cover Main: A 1920s view of Chirk Aqueduct

Page 2: Horse-drawn boats - what the canal was meant for

Page 3: Pleasure Cruising - today's role of the Llangollen Canal

Introduction

This is a book of images of what is today known as the Llangollen Canal. The longest surviving part of the line of the waterway proposed as the Ellesmere Canal, running from its junction with the main line of the Shropshire Union Canal at Hurleston for just over 46 miles to the Horseshoe Falls on the River Dee above Llangollen. It is now the most popular leisure cruising waterway in the UK and also has a world-wide reputation among holiday visitors to this country, especially for the famous Pontcysyllte Aqueduct; currently the central feature of a bid for World Heritage status for the section of canal from Gledrid to Llantysilio.

The book is a collection of some of my photographs taken over the last 48 years whilst first holidaying on the canal, then being involved with it in the boating industry and later as a waterway photographer and journalist. It includes other interesting pictures which are part of our Waterway Images library or have been loaned by others. It is not a technical history of the Ellesmere Canal, although it does contain information and recollections recounted to me by those who have worked on this waterway; some of which are previously unpublished.

The official seal of the Ellesmere Canal Company

Although I have written professionally about waterway history for over 40 years I do not claim to be an historian. I prefer to consider myself as an observer, recorder and – in many cases – collector of waterway history; leaving a detailed study of the Ellesmere Canal and the other constituents that became the Shropshire Union Railway & Canal Company to others. However, if you wish to know more about the section of the Ellesmere Canal which has become part of what is now known as the Montgomery Canal, you may wish to read my book *The Montgomery Canal and its Restoration*.

The images generally run in a sequence following the canal uphill from Hurleston to Llangollen – divided into convenient chapters – but the order sometimes varies to suit the book's layout. Any mistakes, or contentious opinions, are entirely mine, probably brought about by my enthusiasm for and love of this waterway.

The Llangollen Canal – A brief history

It is perhaps surprising that the waterway was called the Ellesmere Canal as, although meetings of the promoters were held in the town, the favoured line – from an obscure village on the Mersey estuary called Netherpool (to become Ellesmere Port) via Chester, Wrexham, Ruabon, Frankton and on to Shrewsbury – wasn't planned to pass through Ellesmere. This was originally just one of many proposed routes, but it was the one favoured by prominent engineer William Jessop who was called in as a consultant.

It was the line approved by the 1793 Act for the Ellesmere Canal, despite the fact that it included some very difficult engineering, including major crossings of the Cerriog and Dee river valleys and an ambitious 4,607-yard tunnel under the hills between Chester and Wrexham. Jessop was appointed engineer, with Thomas Telford as general agent and Thomas Denson, John Duncombe and William Turner as assistants. It was to be built as a narrow canal.

Despite this, the Wirral Line – completed in 1795 – from the Mersey to the Dee at Chester was built to the same broad gauge as the existing Chester Canal, with which it made a junction two years later. Construction at the southern end created an end-on junction with the new Montgomeryshire Canal at Carreghofa by 1797, Chirk Aqueduct was built by 1801 and – after the design of the Dee Valley crossing was finalised in 1795 – the great Pontcysyllte Aqueduct was completed by 1805.

During this period the promoters had a rethink. Other waterway developments around Shrewsbury made them abandon the line south to that town at Weston in 1797 and in 1800 they gave up the idea

Plan of the FOREBAY of the narrow LOCKS for the Ellesmere Canal

One of the few extant construction drawings for the canal, signed by William Jessop in 1794. If Jessop concerned himself with such minor detail, surely he must have had a major input into the design of the big engineering works?

of a main line via Wrexham. The only piece to be cut was the two-mile Ffrwd Branch in 1796. As water supply would be a problem, a feeder canal was cut from Trefor through Llangollen to Llantysilio, tapping the Dee and its main source at Bala Lake via a new weir.

 What was proposed as a branch from Frankton – but would become the main line – was started in 1787, to go via Ellesmere and Whitchurch to join the Chester Canal at Hurleston near Nantwich. There were arms into the town centres of Ellesmere and Whitchurch and a branch to Wem, which actually only ran for just over 3 miles to Quina Brook. All of this was completed by 1811. An amalgamation with the Chester Canal created the Ellesmere & Chester Canal Company, which built a branch to the Trent & Mersey Canal in 1833. A new line from the south – the Birmingham & Liverpool Junction Canal – joined it in 1835 and amalgamated under the same name in 1845.

 With the coming of the railways the Shropshire Union Railway & Canal Company conglomerate was created, then leased and then bought by the London & North Western Railway Company (LNWR) in 1857. Some decline followed, but the LNWR encouraged canal services into Wales – the territory of their rival, the Great

Western Railway – up to the end of the First World War. The LNWR and the Shropshire Union canal network passed into the hands of the London, Midland & Scottish (LMS) Railway Company in 1923. An unrepaired breach severed the canal south of Frankton in 1936 and in 1944 the LMS obtained an Act of Parliament to legally abandon all of the Shropshire Union system except the main line and the Middlewich Branch.

At nationalisation in 1948 ownership passed to the Docks & Inland Waterways Executive which – as it has gone through so many re-namings and reorganisations – I will simply in future call British Waterways or BW. Although officially abandoned, the line up to Llantysilio remained intact as a water feed to the main line and was navigable with difficulty. It was now becoming known as the 'Llangollen Canal' as distinct from the now semi-derelict line from Frankton to Newtown – which became known as the 'Montgomery Canal'. But – proving you can't keep a beautiful waterway closed – through a vigorous ongoing restoration campaign, over half of the latter is again open.

So what saved the Llangollen Canal? Following the publication of Tom Rolt's seminal work *Narrow Boat* in 1944 came a revolution – a rapidly increasing enthusiasm for cruising the waterways for pleasure. The infant Inland Waterways Association campaigned – nationally and through its North West Branch – against proposals to lower bridges and some early members, such as the Grundy family, regularly used it in small cruisers. Since 1935 the pioneering Chester based Inland Hire Cruisers had been encouraging holiday hirers to 'Float Through the Welsh Mountains'.

However, British Transport Waterways then North West Division Engineer, Christopher Marsh, always claimed that it was his 1955 agreement with the Mid & South East Cheshire Water Board to allow them to draw and treat water from the canal at Hurleston Reservoir that secured the future of the Llangollen Canal. Certainly the increasing requirement for this water supply has meant that probably more money has been spent on channel lining and repairs than any comparable 46 miles of BW waterway. By the mid-1960s the immediate connecting canals had probably the greatest concentration of holiday hire boat bases than anywhere else on BW waterways; all claiming to be ideal for the Llangollen Canal. It was already the most popular canal in the country and has remained so.

A final note on history. Perhaps the most interesting aspect is the engineering and the oft asked question is – who did what – Telford or Jessop; particularly with regard to the design of Pontcysyllte Aqueduct? Telford was a great engineer but also a great self-promoter and for the details of this argument you should read Charles Hadfield's *Thomas Telford's Temptation*. During the 1960s hundreds of historical plans, drawings, books, and records of the Shropshire Union network were found dumped in a disused BW office at Market Drayton. The author was one of two people who discovered these and saw just some of the quite amazing drawings. Instructions were given to burn many of the working records but the 'interesting' plans and books were taken away. These have never re-appeared in any archive, but I believe that they have not been destroyed and one day will again surface; to possibly throw a complete new light on the Jessop/Telford controversy and on the history of the Llangollen and other canals.

Harry Arnold

Entering the Llangollen Canal from the main line of the Shropshire Union Canal at Hurleston Junction.

Hurleston to Wrenbury

Above: The four locks of the Hurleston flight – flanked by the banks of the reservoir – immediately lift the canal by 34ft. 3in.

Left: By scaling off the Jessop drawing (p 6) it can be established that the locks were built 7ft 6in wide – generous for the nominal 7ft. beam of a narrow canal. With the passage of time however Hurleston has become a 'pinch point' – initially here at the bottom lock – particularly for the owners of some ex-working narrowboats.

The third lock is currently the tight one but presents no problem for modern boats which are built to a beam of 6ft.10in. It is a theory of the author that so many new boats were initially built in the 1960s to this beam dimension – to use the Llangollen Canal – that it has become the accepted norm. Perhaps we should have campaigned for the rebuilding of Hurleston Locks instead?

Undoubtably one of the busiest flights on the waterways, at Hurleston you are likely to meet boat crews of all nationalities. The historic top ground paddle gear at the third lock is one of the last surviving examples of its type on the canal.

Lock 1 seen in the more tranquil days of 1950s when Tom Godwin was moving the ex-Mersey Weaver & Ship Canal Carrying Company motor narrowboat *Sheila* to Northwich. Note again the slightly different versions of the old upright paddle gear.

The lock keeper's cottage and outhouses are in virtually original form, as are the lock gates. Before management of the reservoir passed to the water authority, the Hurleston lock keeper was also reservoir attendant – in charge of water control – and lengthsman, although did have an assistant.

A somewhat boring picture but it does record the spillway into the reservoir when newly rebuilt in the 1950s. The Shropshire Union company raised the walls of the reservoir between 1904 and 1906 with stone brought by boat from Trefor and Llanymynech. A special wharf was built and the stone unloaded on to a railway running around the reservoir for about a mile.

Plain, but elegantly designed, perhaps best describes the canal's brick accommodation bridges; a good number of which have survived in their original state. The first SU company wharf and warehouse on this section was below here at Burland.

Our first taste of the remote autumn beauty of the canal in early October 1960, on a first cruise between Hurleston and Bettisfield; where we had to turn around because it was the time of one of the major breaches above Trevor (see p121). We hardly saw another pleasure boat.

Lift bridges had been painted with a sort of whitewash but by 1960 were a rather attractive cream colour. Today the paint scheme has reverted to mainly white with black trim.

Over 40 years later this section, seen here between the three Baddiley Locks – although busier – has lost none of its beauty and has been further enhanced by the tree growth over the intervening decades.

Approaching and passing through Swanley No.2 Lock is the *Sir Frances Drake*, a hire cruiser with a hull built in the traditional oak and elm timbers of the working wooden canal boats; a type operated by Shropshire Union Cruises in the 1960s and early 70s. In these August 1966 pictures the banks are definitely in need of repair, although a wooden strapping post survives on the lock side and the gates are still grey. Today, the background of each picture would be dominated by a new marina.

In October 1960 Swanley was the only lock where we had to wait for another boat – Alf Owen and his wife coming downhill with the wooden motor maintenance boat *Weaver*.

Asthetically beautiful and easy on the eye, the wild flowers by Swanley Bridge would have been ruthlessly cut down by the old lengthsmen – but today ecology is everything.

Wrenbury Church Lift Bridge is one of three to be negotiated at this popular village. Although seen in good condition here, this particular bridge has suffered from vandalism and was completely rebuilt in 2007.

The small group of dwellings by Swanley Bridge were not quite so desirable in 1966 as nowadays, although the bungalow *Waters Edge* was then the home of friend and great campaigner for the waterways Ray Slack. He as long-time secretary of the old North West Branch of IWA – did much to save this canal. There was also a lock house for the keeper for the two Swanley Locks, unfortunately long demolished, and the village was also served by a privately-owned wharf.

Head down for the skipper whilst passing under Wrenbury Church Lift Bridge. The clearances for these bridges – and the standard arched types – are given on a standard LMS railway plan (see p1) although the suggested depth of 4ft. 6in. would seem ambitious to anyone using this canal. In working days it was only rated as an '18-ton canal' – that is skippers were paid for this smaller tonnage as a full boat load.

Wrenbury is one of the most historic villages on the canal and – with its two pubs – one of the most popular. Sumner's Mill – seen (above) just after it had been taken over by a boat company – was very attractively adapted by English County Cruises (below) and is now one of the ABC Leisure group's hire bases.

Wrenbury Bridge is one of the biggest and busiest lift bridges – in both boat and road traffic terms. It used to be raised by a winch but after extensive rebuilding it was converted to push-button electro-hydraulic operation. Unfortunately, during this work, the channel was mistakenly re-aligned which now makes the approach rather awkward.

Immediately above the village is the third lift bridge Wrenbury Frith. Horse *Bonny* – towing the restored Shropshire Union fly-boat *Saturn* is taking the passage of it in her stride.

Close encounters with bridges and tunnels encouraged the practice by some hire operators of fitting bars at the fore end, as can be seen on the boat crossing the open countryside above Wrenbury in May 1981.

Marbury Lock is some distance from the pretty village it is named after and is always identifiable by the iron railings alongside the cottage; corralling the lock keeper's children as they chat to the family on an outboard-powered hire boat in this 1968 picture.

The cottage still housed a BW employee in 2003 – although not a lock keeper – and the outside privy building still survives; but the original top paddle gear has gone and the road bridge replaced by an ugly flat deck. Boat styles have also changed somewhat.

Marbury in Marbury Lock: the historic horse-drawn ice boat passes though in 1968 after acquisition by the Shropshire Union Canal Society (see also pp146-147)

Quoisley Lock is right next to the main A49 road and BW took the opportunity to boldly advertise the Llangollen Canal with one of the last surviving of this style of wooden notices on the waterway. Obviously someone thought that a handy lettering kit was a good investment.

Perhaps the most astonishing transformation of any lock location is the once remote Willymoor. When we first passed though in 1960 there was no bridge and the most notable feature was a notice requesting you to leave the lock empty as it leaked into the cottage.

Nowadays any liquid is likely to eminate within the building, as the cottage has been enlarged and converted into a thriving and most welcome pub; not only serving canal users but with full access from the main road.

Grindley Brook – with its flight of three single locks and its trade mark three-lock staircase – is one of the best-known locations on the waterway network. A small community surrounds what was a major wharf here at the bottom lock; the warehouse – converted to modern use-is on the right. There is also the first of two canalside shops on the lock flight and convenient access to the pub and a garage on the main road.

At the top of the staircase is the original Telford designed lock keeper's residence. With its bowed colonnaded verandah it is probably the most attractive and elegant house on the canal.

There can be queues at busy times – a complete contrast with our first 1961 passage, pictured below. Instructions on working the flight must be followed carefully and there is generally a lock keeper (albeit now seasonal) on hand. The fly-boat crews simply worked the staircase uphill by draining everything off, opening the top paddles, and as the water cascaded down to fill each chamber, moved the boat forward, using the water to slam the gates shut behind it. A technique not now approved of by BW but still used on staircase locks in France.

In October 1960 the adjacent mill – now a hotel – was still at work. Cargos of animal feed were once loaded at the top of the locks for various destinations on the Shropshire Union network. The lock keepers doubled as wharfingers and also controlled a water feed coming in at the top.

One of the historic features, seen in the top picture, was the complicated ribbed brickwork which gave a foothold for both boatmen and horses; much of which was damaged when the staircase lock walls had to be extensively rebuilt during the winter of 1969-70.

Above Grindley Brook the canal follows the contours towards, but skirts around, the town of Whitchurch and is crossed by a number of closely spaced bridges – including two carrying the recently built town bypass. The three lift bridges – although themselves somewhat modernised – are a much more attractive sight.

This postcard view of New Mills Lift Bridge – by the entrance to the then open Whitchurch Arm – is one of the earliest illustrations we have seen of one of these bridges in possibly original form. Note the hefty strapping post to assist horse-drawn boats negotiating the tight turn into the arm. Contrast it with this perhaps practical but ugly replacement of Hassell's No.1 Bridge, complete with hand-wound hydraulic operation, designed by a BW engineer. Fortunately, heritage regulations have now ruled out practices such as this.

Perhaps in some mitigation for the ugly replacement, Hassell's No.1 Lift Bridge was in a pretty parlous state in August 1987. Lift bridges varied in detail design; note the simple handrails linked to the chains on this version.

The Whitchurch Arm

This superb 1930s snapshot of Whitchurch Basin – the original town centre terminus of the Whitchurch Arm – actually illustrates early leisure use of the canal. Not only the children fishing, but the *Cuckmere* – one of two used by the then Whitchurch Warehousing Company – was also available for holiday hire; with crew and horse. There are a number of good accounts from past members of parties who hired the boats from here.

Whitchurch Arm 'now filled in' – as the first BW blue guide described it – and as we viewed the stretch by Chemistry Farm from the main canal in 1960. Three years later we would winter a boat horse here.

Who then would have forseen a campaign to re-connect the town with the main canal? But along came the enthusiasts of the Whitchurch Waterways Trust and this is today's view from exactly the same location; taken during one of the Trust's popular annual festivals.

Another pair of comparison views, this time looking back towards the main canal from Chemistry Farm. Excavation is in hand during September 1993 and later boats fill the re-watered section of the Arm.

The Arm is believed to have been disused by the start of World War II and these pictures of filling in the section by Chemistry Farm were taken in 1955. The infilling work was done by BW and George Elliot is driving the Marshall tractor.

The view from Chemistry Bridge which – unlike the others on the Arm – remains intact and is currently the limit of navigation.

These four hand coloured postcards are from a series published in Whitchurch by a local man Thomas J.H.Purcell: possibly he was the photographer. They provide a fascinating record of parts of the 1-mile Arm when – judging by the immaculate towpath – it was a working waterway. Traffic was extensive, not only to a busy canal company wharf and cheese warehouse, but to coal wharves and a mill.

Whitchurch Market – seen below during a mid-week Cheese Fair day – was perhaps the most important local source of canal traffic in Shropshire Union days. Special 'Fair boats' (or 'Cheese Flys') would be waiting to deliver cheese from the fairs (also held in turn at Market Drayton and Nantwich) to the markets in Manchester and for export from Liverpool, via Ellesmere Port. Cheese Flys were specially fitted with numbered shelves and double top cloths – including one of linen and another of heavy white material to keep the sun's heat out – with a grill in the cratch for air circulation. Cheeses were stacked two high on the shelves.

Beyond the current limit of navigation at Chemistry Bridge the Whitchurch Waterways Trust has a number of reopening problems. On the other side of this new bridge – which appears to provide navigable clearance – much of the old line has been built over. A completely new route into the town is planned which could involve the building of an inclined plane.

Despite the filling-in of the terminal basin a number of the original surrounding buildings survived until the area was eventually cleared in November 2004 for the inevitable 'redevelopment'; just retaining the single canal warehouse in the left background.

Whixhall Moss is quite the most remote section of the waterway and in certain weather conditions the crossing can be quite an eerie experience. It is a peat bog and now a Site of Special Scientific Interest.

Tilstock Park is now well-known for its attractively sited lift bridge and nearby house but it was once the site of a busy stone wharf and kilns burning lime for local agriculture.

In September 1961 horse *Mary* is about to confuse two approaching early hire cruisers from the Wolverhampton company of Double Pennant as she tows the hostelboat *Margaret* across Whixhall Moss. Keeping the water in has always been a problem on the Moss and many old wooden narrowboats, loaded with stone and clay, have been sunk along this stretch in the past.

Platt Lane Bridge and its distinctive house were once also the site of a private wharf and warehouse. It seems remote, and there is a welcome, but equally isolated pub, The *Waggoners* just up the road to the right.

As the canal has been raised above the shrinking peat Morris's Lift Bridge, seen here in May 1982, stands proud above the surrounding countryside.

The cottage at Lyneal Wharf was donated by IWA past national chairman John Heap and his wife Joan to The Lyneal Trust who now operate land and water based holidays for those with special needs from here. HRH Princess Alexandra is seen officially naming the Trust's first boat on 15 July 1987.

As the 'Shropshire Lake District' around Ellesmere approaches, the countryside becomes more wooded. A typical early quality canal cruiser, built for a private owner by Dobsons of Shardlow, passes a day boat in this early 1970s picture.

Cole Mere is to the left as a classic steam launch passes an equally classic hire boat from English County Cruises. What is now Colemere Country Park was once a small centre of industry with a stone wharf, lime kilns and a mill at the nearby Little Mill Bridge.

There is a small ridge, carrying the Shrewsbury Road, barring the approach to Ellesmere that necessitated the building of a short tunnel and an approach cutting.

In September 1961 Jack Roberts hold the *Margaret* steady at the downstream portal whilst he checks that the tunnel is clear.

Although the 87-yard Ellesmere Tunnel has a towpath it was the general practice in horse-boating days to walk the horse over the top, to giving its shoulders a rest after the long haul along the 13-mile lock free stretch from Grindley Brook. Oakmere Wharf, for the Oakley Estate, was situated here.

Somewhat short of the town, perhaps the most idyllic mooring for the mere country is here along Blake Mere where very little land separates the two areas of water.

The elegant but unusually named Red Bridge once heralded your arrival at Ellemere, but nowadays the approach is signified by a major marina just downstream of it. Also, even in winter, stopping in the bridge hole to load up – as the hostel boat *Aston* was doing in December 1964 – would be most unlikely.

The Prees Branch

One of the longest of the canal's arms was the Prees Branch – called by working boatmen the 'Wem Canal'. It left the main canal at Whixhall Moss Roving Bridge and ran for 3.6 miles to a wharf on the Whitchurch to Wem road at Quina Brook. By the early 1900s it was shallow, although still used commercially. The first third has remained navigable with the modern terminus at Whixhall Marina and the next part – still in water – remaining as a nature reserve. One of the two lift bridges is the assembly point for a Shropshire Union Canal Society work party in July 1968.

The entrance to the branch seen from Whixhall Moss Roving Bridge in September 1961 and the weedy state of the supposed navigable section in July 1968.

One of the reasons that part of the Branch remained navigable was that just south of Dobson's Bridge was the main source of good puddling clay on the canal – a 'clay 'ole' as the boatmen called it – now Whixhall Marina. There was a tramway, with trucks wire-rope hauled by a static engine, ending in a tippler dropping the clay into maintenance boats. With a loaded truck c1955 are (l to r) George Guest, Jack Roberts, Jim Jones and George Levy. Shortly after the top picture was taken the method of digging and moving clay went over to dragline excavator and lorries.

Swans glide under Waterloo Bridge in July 1968, where the water was stanked off and there was once a wharf. The last mile was called by the boatmen the 'Wrens Nest' and served Edstaston Wharf - seen here at the same time – which had a coal warehouse one side and a stone warehouse on the other. There was also a coal wharf, lime kilns and a pub called the *Harp Inn* at the terminus of the Branch. Prior to 1920 the wharves were served by Shropshire Union company boats and among others, those of Griffiths Brothers, corn merchants of Chester and those of the Cerriog Granite Company.

Restored Shropshire Union Fly-boat *Saturn* recalls the past arrivals of such a boat at the junction with the Ellesmere Arm – although in the heyday of the fly-boat services the boat would have had an all-male crew. If they had no goods to deliver to the town wharf the fly-boats would not go down the Arm unless they were ordered to collect cargo by a notice displayed here at White Bridge.

Virtually all that now remains of the once extensive commercial development surrounding the Arm is the crane and the warehouse. Ellesmere was another centre of cheese production and there were a number of wharves, handling a variety of goods, including timber, lime and coal; also a gas works, a foundry and latterly a large dairy company. The whole area to the west of the Arm is currently being radically changed by redevelopment.

What is now known as Beech House was built as the original headquarters of the Ellesmere Canal Company in 1805-6. The bowed section which dominates the junction was the committee room. It remained the main administrative centre until the formation of the Shropshire Union Railway & Canal Company in 1846.

Passing Beech House in the 1930s is pioneer pleasure boater William Eaton Parker on his boat *Tramp*. Liverpool born, he owned a shipyard at Dinas on the Menai Straits, from which he transported *Tramp* by horse-drawn cart and railway to launch it at Chirk.

A familiar sight – in December 1964 - moored at Beech House was Dennis Hobson-Greenwood's handsome cruiser. His father bought the ex-Shropshire Union management inspection boat *Inspector*, which was based at Ellesmere, and had it converted and motorised at Frankton Dock; renaming it *Hobsons Choice*. It was broken up at Ellesmere just after World War II. Dennis and his cruiser are still happily enjoying the canals.

The warehouse at the end of the Ellesmere Arm – with its splendid company slogan – is one of the finest survivors of its type on the Shropshire Union network. Seen here when the dairy was in full production – hence the parked lorries – let us hope that at least the basic structure survives intact in the redevelopment of the area.

Another historic gem is the British Waterways' yard – started in 1807 – and still working and serving as the central maintenance depot for the canal. The lock gate shop is superb and in September 1961 we saw the last set of wooden lock gates being made before manufacture (in steel) was centralised at Northwich.

Forty-six years later the shop is still being used for quality construction work with the building of part of the new Wrenbury Church Lift Bridge in hand. Timber is now back in vogue for both lift bridges and lock gates.

In the 1950s Jack Roberts' horse *Molly* stands contentedly on the towpath whilst his boat (probably the *Antwerp*) is at the yard by the side of the dry dock. A spot where pleasure boaters now fill their boats with water and empty their toilets.

Section Inspector Stan Hughes checks out a newly completed wide lock gate. Ellesmere made gates for all parts of the north west area and they were moved by boat, the wide gates carried vertically in the hold; a difficult cargo to balance. Apparently they just cleared the bridges. Note the elaborate overhead crane system that ran from the shop to the water.

In the late 1940s and early 50s there were generally 20-25 men actually working in the yard; comprising of 2-3 in the office, 2 blacksmiths and their strikers, a fitter and his apprentice, 5 or 6 joiners, 2 sawyers, 2 painter/plumbers, 2 boatbuilders, a boilerman, a lorry driver and a chap who kept the place clean. Some of the men seen here working on lock gates are Arnold Whitaker, Ray Keen and Tom Barkley. The latter had a long waterway career, retiring as a waterway supervisor on the Trent & Mersey Canal.

Despite the modern machinery, this 2006 view of the joiner's shop still has a Victorian air about it; the main thing missing being the original belt drives from the line shafts driven by a steam engine. Timber was also bought and cut at Ellesmere to be sent by boat to the company's main boatbuilding yard at Chester.

The yard's dry dock was also a gauging dock, that is boats were measured by putting in standard weights for the future calculation of tolls. In this September 1961 picture the cranes for lowering in the weights are still in place.

By the time of this 2007 view of *Saturn* on the dock the cranes and the fascinating clutter of timber have gone and – in deference to Health & Safety regulations – the edges now have rails. However, some of the gauging weights still exist including this early Ellesmere Canal Company example (inset).

Above Ellesmere, for the three miles to Frankton Junction, the canal assumes a remote winding nature avoiding the village of Tetchill, although there were small warehouses and wharves serving local farms at Coachman's, Val Hill and Broom bridges.

Frankton is the junction with what is now known as the Montgomery Canal, which is now open again from here to beyond the village of Maesbury. It was still derelict in August 1957 when *Saturn* – then recently converted to an hotel boat – moored up here. Passing is one of the earliest purpose-built canal cruisers by Holt-Abbott of Stourport.

On the corner at Frankton was a transhipment wharf and warehouse for goods from boats going to different destinations towards Newtown or Llangollen. When it was dismantled the ever parsimonious canal company made the warehouse part of Lyneal Wharf cottage and sold the shed in the foreground to Oswestry Cattle Market; where it stood well into the 1980s.

In Shropshire Union days the left turn down to Newtown was still considered the main canal and the line straight on to Llantysilio entitled on official distance tables the 'Pontcysylte Branch' (the latter with a single 'l' spelling). So the bridge numbering sequence carried on down toward Newtown, then straight ahead started afresh with Rowsons Bridge as No.1; something which confuses modern pleasure boaters; especially as for some reason in guides to the canal it has now acquired the number 70!

In contrast to the summer holiday atmosphere on the opposite page, this January 1977 picture shows Frankton Junction in the grip of winter; although both maintenance and pleasure boats are still on the move.

Unfortunately for early users – and unlike many other canals – pubs right on the waterside were fairly rare on this canal, until that is various entrepreneurs opened new and welcoming hostelries, such as Colin Hill's *Narrowboat Inn*, here by the main Oswestry – Ellesmere Road at Maestermyn.

At New Marton are the final two locks on the waterway. The top lock was also a toll collection point and the lock house also a toll office. William Clay was one of the toll collectors and these pictures of his family and some local friends – all in their 'Sunday best' – are believed to have been taken about 1905.

Horse *Mary* pulls the hostel boat *Margaret* between the two New Marton locks in September 1961. The Margaret was built for millers A & A Peate at Maesbury and this length of waterway was the nearest she ever got to her original home; being scrapped before the Montgomery Canal was reopened to that point.

The New Marton Locks raise the waterway 12ft. 4in. to its 13–mile summit level through to the River Dee at Llantysilio. Another job for the lock keeper here was to record the daily water levels. There was a major culvert collapse at New Marton Lock 2 in 1909 when a wooden trough was built at Ellesmere Yard and installed to get canal open quicker. As with other breaches in those days boatmen who were trapped were employed on the repairs.

New Marton Bridge not only provides wide vistas of Shropshire scenery but the first real view of the not so distant Welsh hills. In some early Shropshire Union company publications the location is spelled 'Martin' – with an 'I' - similar to the next village.

The cottage on the right (which the author once leased) on the approach to the village of St Martin's was the last resting place of the fly-boat *Antwerp*. In a quite remarkably feat the boat was pulled out sideways into the extremely narrow garden to be used as a chicken shed, then gradually sawn up.

The surviving buildings by St Martin's Moor Bridge give something of a clue that this was once a busy wharf, but the tranquillity masks the fact that this was also once a busy part of the North Shropshire coalfield and a tramway brought coal down to the canal just upstream of here.

Chirk Aqueduct

Quite suddenly – as the canal twists through Rhoswiel and into the valley of the River Ceriog alongside the original A5 road at Chirk Bank – you are confronted by the first of the canal's two great aqueduct at Chirk.

At 68ft. high, when Chirk Aqueduct was built in 1800 it was for a while the world's highest canal aqueduct and – as this early print shows – was not then overshadowed by the later 106ft. high railway viaduct.

As far as we know the camera never captured this period scene of the fly-boat *Symbol* crossing the aqueduct – with a steam train on the viaduct – created by artist Dusty Miller for the Shropshire Union Fly-boat Restoration Society.

The camera did however record this early picture of the maintenance boat *Starling* on the aqueduct, believed to be carrying clay to Trevor It is thought to date from 1927/8 and the print is from the original Leica negative in the author's collection; which – as the Leica camera was only first produced shortly before this date – makes it interesting photographically. Just to add to the detail – the skipper is Jack Evans, the mate Tom Price, the dog *Jip* and the horse *Big John*. It is interesting to compare it with the modern view below.

Chirk is also unusual in that – to reduce weight - the arch spans are hollow and the canal is carried in an iron trough. It was originally built with an iron bottom plate and supposedly waterproof masonry sides but there were problems with leaks. A report of 30 December 1868 recommended the fixing of iron sides to the bottom plate, but eventually the company who did the job scrapped the existing bottom plate and put in a complete new iron trough. According to the report on the work by engineer G.R. Jebb of 29 September 1869, the trough installation was "begun on the morning of 20 September and finished Saturday 25 September". An amazing feat of engineering even by modern standards.

These pictures were taken when the author was allowed inside the aqueduct in December 1977 with consulting engineers who were inspecting serious defects caused by water seeping through the structure, not from the canal but rain water filtering through the towpath and offside edges; possibly a fault started by the company who fitted the trough literally stuffing the sides with rubble. It was somewhat un-nerving – to say the least – that when standing on the arches you could see the valley below between the gaps in the stonework. You could also see remaining jagged edges of iron where the original bottom plate had been broken out.

Somewhat undignified, but the only way to climb inside a hollow aqueduct, head first as in potholing. Each arch has access holes at the springing but you need scaffolding to reach them.

This August 1976 view from the railway side show the state of the unsealed offside edge through which rain water had seeped for over 100 years causing – among other things – the outer walls of the arches to bulge.

By June 1983 – with the top edges sealed and the stonework re-pointed – the ten-arch structure can be seen again in all its original glory.

Following the lead of Eric de Maré every serious photographer of this canal takes this shot over the basin and along the aqueduct from Chirk Tunnel top. Following the lead of a great photographer doesn't make it any less satisfying.

The outs and ins of the 459yd. Chirk Tunnel, the longest on the canal; which can be another bottleneck when things are busy. By the southern portal is a good mooring for visiting Chirk Castle, a not-to-be-missed attraction of the Llangollen Canal.

Tramp and the Eaton Parkers have Chirk Basin to themselves in the 1930s. Apart from launching the boat here, after transporting it by rail from the Menai Strait, they owned a piece of land at Chirk.

Beyond the tunnel, Chirk cutting was always a problem with slipping sides and falling trees. In the winter of 1997/8 British Waterways undertookextensive remedial works which – due to lack of access – necessitated excavators working in the water.

In a somewhat more summery mood, hotel boats *Jupiter* and *Saturn* cruise through the cutting. The Shropshire Union company owned the adjacent Glyn Valley Tramway which had an interchange station with the main line at Chirk and a coal loading wharf from Black Park Colliery, for both canal and railway, at the north end of the cutting.

Hotel boat *Jupiter* emerges from the 191yd. Whitehouse Tunnel, the last of the three on the canal.

Below the village of Froncysyllte the canal now runs in a concrete channel as this stretch also had serious leakage problems. There were a number of lime kilns at the wharf here.

In 1966 there was no concrete and far fewer trees to block the view of the impressive railway viaduct that spans the Dee Valley.

The same boat negotiates Fron Lift Bridge. As the notice instructs, the boater had to open it by throwing a line over the counter weight to pull it down.

Similar nautical dexterity with a line was also required in September 1961 when the *Margaret* and an Ernest Thomas hire boat from Gailey passed through. Running on to the bridge was also a required technique to tip the balance and close it.

Now the attractive wooden bridge has been replaced by an ugly steel version – mounted on the other bank – and flanked by an equally characterless footbridge. The passage of the ex-Grand Union Canal Carrying Company's boat *Star* illustrates that – despite the width problems at Hurleston Locks – some 'big' motor narrowboats can navigate most of this canal.

Jupiter and *Saturn* round the turn at the Froncysyllte winding hole in September 1972. This is now quite a busy spot as the boat trips across the aqueduct turn here.

Because it is largely tree covered and the presence of Pontcysyllte Aqueduct rather overshadows it, this long southern approach embankment to the Dee crossing is somewhat overlooked as a feat of engineering. It is in fact a massive earthwork and has been the root of some serious problems – particularly where it connects with the aqueduct – as a drawing of past remedial works in the author's collection illustrates.

Pontcysyllte Aqueduct

The world-famous aqueduct is an awesome sight from any angle but perhaps you need to stand back – in the field below or on the river bridge – to appreciate the 1,007ft. length and the 126ft. 8in. height.

Pontcysyllte immediately became a popular subject for many early engravings and prints and you need to go to the print section of the National Museum of Wales to see a full selection. Even the gentry were anxious to demonstrate that it could be viewed from their grand houses, as in the one below entitled *Vale of Llangollen – From the Tower, Wynnstay Park* and dated c.1836.

The spelling varied somewhat and this undated and uncredited one in the author's collection is entitled *Pont-Y-Casullte Aqueduct – In the Vale of Llangollen*, Denbighshire. It may however be a variation on an engraving from drawing by George Yates which was presented to the canal company directors at the opening ceremony and has the same spelling.

From the first days of pleasure boating on this canal, hire companies promoted the thrills of cruising at such a height. In this early shot from the river bridge a boat from Inland Hire Cruisers fully justifies their 'Float through the Welsh Mountains' marketing slogan.

Photographed in my favourite lighting conditions – when the setting sun shining down the Vale of Llangollen turns the locally quarried grey Cefn Mawr stone of the aqueduct's pillars to gold.

The first of hundreds of Pontcysyllte pictures. Taken of the Margaret crossing in October 1961, when the horse had to be walked around the road because the towpath was closed. This transparency is so badly damaged by various printers that I thought it unusable, but such are the modern marvels of PhotoShop!

One of the most common camera positions – ideal for shortening the aqueduct's length – is from by the cottage on the road down to the river bridge from Trevor. It also gives time to vary the position of the boat.

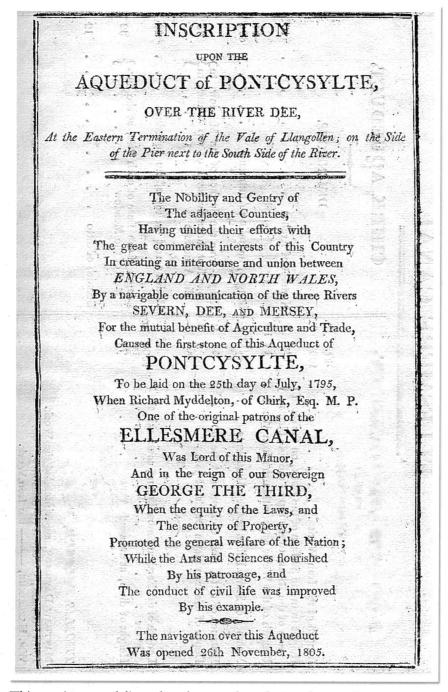

INSCRIPTION

UPON THE

AQUEDUCT of PONTCYSYLTE,

OVER THE RIVER DEE,

At the Eastern Termination of the Vale of Llangollen; on the Side of the Pier next to the South Side of the River.

The Nobility and Gentry of
The adjacent Counties,
Having united their efforts with
The great commercial interests of this Country
In creating an intercourse and union between
ENGLAND AND NORTH WALES,
By a navigable communication of the three Rivers
SEVERN, DEE, AND MERSEY,
For the mutual benefit of Agriculture and Trade,
Caused the first-stone of this Aqueduct of
PONTCYSYLTE,
To be laid on the 25th day of July, 1795,
When Richard Myddelton, of Chirk, Esq. M. P.
One of the original patrons of the
ELLESMERE CANAL,
Was Lord of this Manor,
And in the reign of our Sovereign
GEORGE THE THIRD,
When the equity of the Laws, and
The security of Property,
Promoted the general welfare of the Nation;
While the Arts and Sciences flourished
By his patronage, and
The conduct of civil life was improved
By his example.

The navigation over this Aqueduct
Was opened 26th November, 1805.

This oration was delivered at the aqueduct during the opening ceremony on 26 November 1805 and was also a page in a 'Report to The General Assembly of The Ellesmere Canal Proprietors' presented at a meeting held at the Royal Oak Inn, Ellesmere, on the following day. If you want to see the version cast in iron, the plaque is mounted on the pillar that stands right in the centre of the River Dee (opposite); perhaps an early anti-vandalism measure?

THE NOBILITY AND
THE ADJACENT COUNTIES,
HAVING UNITED THEIR EFFORTS WITH
THE GREAT COMMERCIAL INTEREST OF THIS COUNTRY,
IN CREATING AN INTERCOURSE AND UNION BETWEEN
ENGLAND AND NORTH WALES,
BY A NAVIGABLE COMMUNICATION OF THE THREE RIVERS,
SEVERN, DEE AND MERSEY,
FOR THE MUTUAL BENEFIT OF AGRICULTURE AND TRADE;
CAUSED THE FIRST STONE OF THIS AQUEDUCT OF
PONTCYSYLLTE
TO BE LAID ON THE 25TH DAY OF JULY M, DCC, XCV,
WHEN RICHARD MYDDELTON, OF CHIRK, ESQ. M.P.
ONE OF THE ORIGINAL PATRONS OF THE
ELLESMERE CANAL,
WAS LORD OF THIS MANOR,
AND IN THE REIGN OF OUR SOVEREIGN
GEORGE THE THIRD
WHEN THE EQUITY OF THE LAWS, AND
THE SECURITY OF PROPERTY,
PROMOTED THE GENERAL WELFARE OF THE NATION;
WHILE THE ARTS AND SCIENCES FLOURISHED
BY HIS PATRONAGE, AND
THE CONDUCT OF CIVIL LIFE WAS IMPROVED
BY HIS EXAMPLE

It is not an illusion created by the camera, the 18 piers do taper towards their full height of 116ft. and – to keep the overall weight down – were built partly hollow for the last 50ft. The 19 cast iron arches each span 45ft. and the sections were assembled with a waterproofing sandwich of Welsh flannel soaked in a mixture of boiled sugar and lead; then the joints were caulked on the outside in the same manner as a wooden boat. The first stone was laid on 25 July 1975 and £47,018 was the total bill for the aqueduct's construction.

In another detailed re-creation of a pre-First World War scene by artist Dusty Miller, the fly-boat *Saturn* is depicted crossing Pontcysyllte, as she would have done when working the 'Llangollen Fly' service. The painting was commissioned by the author's family as a fund-raiser for The Saturn Project and high quality prints are available from the Shropshire Union Fly-boat Restoration Society.

Perhaps *Saturn's* swift and silent progress should be contrasted with the noise of throbbing diesel engines from this queue of modern craft crossing towards Trevor; a not uncommon sight in high summer.

Pulling the plug! It is quite a spectacular sight when the aqueduct has to be stopped off and drained for inspection and/or maintenance work, as here in March 1974; especially as the trough alone holds about a third of a million gallons of water which takes about 2 hours to cascade into the river. There are pumps at the aqueduct, raising the water directly from the Dee and keeping the supply going down the canal to Hurleston.

The round plug is located in the bottom of the trough over the river and is operated – via a cranked lever mechanism – by this firmly secured handle.

An empty aqueduct, seen before a clean-out. The water channel width is 11ft. 8in. and the towpath is cantilevered over it by 4ft. Much remedial and restoration work has been done since this picture was taken in February 1989.

Pontcysyllte Aqueduct's bicentenary was celebrated on Saturday 26 November 2005 – 200 years to the day from when the structure was first opened and a culmination of a year of events. During a very memorable day of re-enactments and other festivities the Inland Waterways Association presented British Waterways with an illuminated proclamation – marking the occasion and signed by senior representatives of local authorities along the length of the original Ellesmere Canal. BW chief executive Robin Evans received it from IWA vice president Martin Grundy. It was most appropriate that Martin should present this as he and his family were probably the longest serving campaigners for the future of this waterway present at the celebration.

The opening of the event was a grand procession of boats across the aqueduct carrying representatives of many organisations and led by *Saturn* with the VIPs aboard. Their arrival at Trevor triggered the rain, but fortunately it was just a shower and certainly not sufficient to dampen the enthusiasm of the re-enactors – including these military gentlemen in period dress – and the large crowds who turned out to watch.

Despite the 'its as good as the day it was built' claims over the years, Pontcysyllte Aqueduct was not. Only regular maintenance and repairs over 200 years has kept it in good order; the last bill for the extensive 2003/4 refurbishment being £2.3 million. In 1975 it was found that the two internal girders supporting the southernmost arch had failed and these had to be replaced by steel versions. The damaged ones are seen here being erected as an exhibit outside the National Waterways Museum, Stoke Bruerne.

Big holes can be seen in the towpath during our second crossing with the *Margaret* during September 1961. The path was gated off with barbed wire but it didn't prevent the locals swinging around the obstructions (with their bikes!) and carrying on using it. A new surface was laid on a supporting bed of trench sheeting, which has since been removed and a proper restoration job done.

Can he trust the strength of those railings? A bit of illegal abseiling from the aqueduct in September 1990. But in late 1987 Northwich area engineer Brian Haskins used this method to carry out a major investigation of the structure. Abseiling engineers of Stats (UK) Ltd took just three days to make a visual and photographic record of the structure.

<u>Trevor to Llangollen</u>

Trevor was one of the earliest bases for self-drive holiday hire boats on this canal. In carrying days it was an important wharf and the agent's office was the existing hire company building, with a six-horse stable located next to it. The current *Telford Inn*, seen in the picture, was not the original pub which was called *The Wharf Tavern*, and apparently renowned for fights between boatmen and the local populace.

Through Scotch Hall Bridge was a further complex of buildings, including canal company cottages and an interesting railway/canal interchange warehouse. Those with an eye for such structures may just be able to recognise it seen through the bridge arch during an Eaton Parker visit with *Tramp* in the 1930s.

Although there are still modern factories within sight there are few physical remains – except the canal arms themselves – to show that this was once a busy complex of industry and wharves. Jack Roberts recalls loading general goods, stone, coal from Ruabon, bricks from J.C. Edwards of Acrefair and various chemicals from Glaciers; which became Monsanto. A lot of munitions were also made and shipped out from here during the First World War. As part of the recent renovation of the aqueduct extensive improvements, including rebuilding the wharf walls, were made to the twin arms.

Navigation at Trevor now ends here. The canal went on however around the edge of valley to serve a number of industrial sites – including the original Ruabon Iron Works – to join the privately owned Plas Kynaston Canal near Cefn-mawr; built in about 1830 and closed by about 1914.

What might have been? The only part of the proposed main line via Wrexham to Chester ever built was the Ffrwd Branch which was started in 1796 and abandoned – after construction of just two miles – in 1798. There is some doubt whether any boats used it but, conversely to its length and obscurity, it seems to attract a lot of interest among canal historians. The diligent researcher can still find the remains of the terminal basin pictured here.

Turning up what was originally built as a water feeder under Rhos-y-Coed Bridge and skirting the edge of Trevor there was, in September 1961, a farm which sold honey by the next (Postles) footbridge

All this was swept away during the winter of 1988/9 by the extensive works to concrete the channel and hopefully finally solve the problems of leaks and bursts. The section from Trevor to Llangollen used to be inspected every morning – seven days a week – and piles of clay were kept to stop leaks by the very narrow section at Llangollen.

The sheer beauty of holiday boating through the lovely Welsh countryside contained in this valley high above the River Dee is no better illustrated than these pictures at Millars and Bryn Howell bridges.

Breaches have been the scourge of this section, with no less than four major bursts and resultant extended closures since World War II. The first of these on 6 September 1945 happened between Sun Trevor and Wenffrwd bridges, washing away the railway line below (now closed) and causing a train wreck which killed the driver and fireman. Just 15 years later, on 5 September 1960 – during our first cruise on the canal – the canal again burst just short of Bryn Ceirch Bridge; in an area to be plagued by further landslips. The resultant hole is pictured above.

On 8 March 1982 the next and third post-war breach happened, again sweeping the canal formation down into the valley. These pictures show British Waterway's Northwich based engineers initially inspecting the damage on the following day. Contractors were brought in to repair the canal and were told at the time by local BW staff that they were using the wrong material to remake the embankment.

The then chairman of the British Waterways Board, Sir Frank Price, officially reopened the canal on 24 June 1983, accompanied by the Mayor of Llangollen. As Llangollen was an established tourist centre, traders initially claimed that closure of the canal made no difference to their business; but this breach rapidly changed their minds.

Perhaps Sir Frank shouldn't have felt so safe, as another collapse, just upstream of the 1982 incident, blew away a large section of the recently-built concrete channel on 22 January 1985. These pictures show local Inland Waterways Association officer Ron Reid inspecting the resulting damage on the following day. This breach led to a major structural survey of the waterway and resulted in extensive and expensive installation of concrete channelling here and on other canal sections in the area.

There were – and have been recently – less serious breaches in the lower section of the canal. The first priority is to keep the water supply flowing. Tom Godwin is seen here operating a tractor-driven pump in a pipe moving water around a breach somewhere near the A5 road in the 1950s.

Nature is now taking over and starting to soften the harsh effect of the concrete in this post-channel reconstruction view.

The banks were not as stable, but the towpath much more attractive, when the *Margaret* was in the Sun Trevor area in the 1961 and 1962. Sun Trevor Wharf was a major loading point for limestone from the quarries in the hills above and there was a tramway crossing the road here to bring the stone down to the canal.

This length below the crossing of the main Wrexham to Llangollen road at Wenffrwd Bridge is described as 'narrow' in the cruising guides; surely a purely comparative term! Stephen and Susan Rees-Jones, supervised by dog *Jethro*, pass through here on their hotel boat *Tsarina* in June 1974.

The original Wenffrwd Bridge crossed the canal at right angles but – because everything has to be subservient to road traffic – on rebuilding they created a difficult bend in the canal. This small cruiser is alright, but Jack Roberts used to offer half-a-crown to anyone who could steer a full-length boat through the bridge without hitting the sides.

Virtually squeezing into Llangollen, with the road, railway, river and town centre below, the waterway and the boats have this rather grand castellated house as an additional scenic backdrop.

One of the oldest waterway businesses – certainly the oldest horse-drawn operation – operates from Llangollen Wharf. Captain Jones, an ex-merchant navy officer, rented the canal company wharf in 1884 and with two ship's lifeboats started to run horse-drawn passenger trips. He expanded to four boats, had rowing boats for hire and also acted as the canal company's agent at the wharf. Today, the trips are still as popular as ever.

Llangollen Wharf appeared to be in very much original condition when Ted Smout ran Welsh Canal Holiday Craft from here in the 1960s, offering one-way cruises to Wheaton Aston on the Shropshire Union main line. Today's summer scene on the wharf very much reflects the current holiday atmosphere of the canal and the town.

Beyond the wharf swans were the only movement disturbing the winding hole when the Eaton Parkers on *Tramp* moored at Llangollen in the 1930s

The wharf buildings underwent a major renovation to accommodate the new Llangollen Canal Exhibition in March 1974.

The Llangollen Canal Exhibition – housed in the wharf building – presented the history of the waterways within a very compact space. It was a pioneer of the concept of story-telling used in today's museums and won the first tourist board 'Come to Britain' award – competing against much larger attractions – and presented by HRH The Prince of Wales. The author – along with others acknowledged for their kind contributions to this book (see p 160) – was involved in its design and construction. Unfortunately it was later moved to another venue to make more commercial use of the space.

Not a view of Llangollen Wharf the tourists normally see - winter snow and the trip boats high and dry because the feed from the Horseshoe Falls is turned off.

Mooring at Llangollen has always been a problem. After years of negotiation with the local authority, British Waterways has managed to construct a purpose-built visitor mooring basin at the limit of navigation for normal craft.

Although the only regular traffic on the feeder for over 100 years has been the horse-drawn trip boats there were wharves along it and commercial craft went up to load stone and slate slabs; which came by tramway from the nearby quarries in the hillsides above.

One of Captain Jones's original boats pauses for a posed photograph. Published as a post card, this is however off an original print, purchased by the author from Friths when they went into liquidation.

The feeder gets narrower as it passes under the final Kings Bridge on the road up to the now reopened Berwyn Station.

Customers at the well-known *Chainbridge Hotel* – which occupies the limited space between the canal and the Dee at this point – watch steam trains cross the Berwyn Viaduct during a gala day on the reopened Llangollen Railway.

Where the Llangollen Canal ends and the feed water comes in from the Dee at Llantysilio. Before the sluices and valves were rebuilt there was a single gate through which boats could pass on to the river. Alf Owen recalls his father taking a boat on to the Dee.

Horseshoe Falls – an example of where a well-engineered, man-made structure can actually enhance the existing natural beauty of a location.

An unusual trip for Jack Robert's father Alfred was to skipper the boat *Ruth* for a number of gentlemen who hired it from the canal company for a trip from Nantwich to Llangollen. Unfortunately the date is unknown. The *Ruth* – seen moored at Bettisfield Wharf – looks rather tired, which is possibly why it could be spared for such an outing.

I'm responsible for all this? Harriet Hudson had the distinction of becoming British Waterways' first female waterway manager when she was put in charge of the Llangollen Canal.

Jack Roberts – seen here giving his daughters Freda and Linda a ride on horse *Molly* – worked for most of his life as a skipper on horse-drawn boats on the Llangollen Canal and waterways north of Birmingham; apart from a spell in the army and on railway maintenance. His grandfather Edward Roberts was born in Bala in 1819 and subsequently left an orphan. On his way to the workhouse he ran off and begged a ride on a boat at Llangollen going to London; starting the family boating tradition on a Pickford's fly then coming back to the Shropshire Union as a skipper. He was drowned at Bettisfield, but Jack's father Alfred Roberts, born in 1862, followed on. Jack was born on the boat *Quail* at Christleton on 29 May 1894 and made his first trip up the Llangollen Canal at age of 10 in 1904 whilst at school. He left school in 1908 to start his boating career.

Jack Roberts' retirement virtually coincided with the demise of horse-drawn maintenance boats on the Llangollen Canal and he later became skipper of the horse-drawn hostel boat *Margaret*. He was a great ambassador for the waterways, instilling in many of us a love for canals which has never diminished and generously passing on his boating skills to those of us who were keen to learn.

The practice of children riding on boat horses was still alive and well when David Martin, mate on the hostel boat *Margaret*, gave each of the lock keeper's children at Hurleston a ride on *Mary* in September 1961.

Jack Robert's father Alfred poses for the camera with his horse *Bobby*. Typical Shropshire Union boatmen's dress was white corduroy trousers, blue waistcoat, blue and white or black neckerchief and blue socks. They also wore shoes with the tongue over the laces specially hand made in Stone and costing 15 shillings a pair; a lot of money in those days. Unlike boatmen in the south they didn't wear the 'spiders-web' belts, but leather belts decorated with small horse brasses, often made in Llangollen; one of which the author still has. In deference to his gentlemen passengers on this trip Alfred Roberts appears to be wearing a collar and tie!

The men of Ellesmere Yard gather round as Section Inspector Stan Hughes makes a retirement presentation to Edgar E. Thomas, the yard fitter (in cap) in about 1952. Edgar was about 71 and had worked there since leaving school at 14 or 15 and was a single man and a keen cyclist. He cycled from Lands End to John o' Groats during one of his holidays but got tired and took a short ride on a train somewhere in Scotland. He was so annoyed with himself afterwards that he cycled the whole distance again in the following year. Noting his age from their records the Liverpool divisional office sent memos to Stan Hughes saying that Edgar should retire; which Stan first ignored as he didn't like to tell him. Stan eventually had him in the office and broke the news and Edgar – big cap in hand – said "If I had known the job wouldn't be permanent I would'na started".

The horse-drawn ice breaker *Marbury* was still in use at Ellesmere Yard in September 1961 but some time later was abandoned and sunk down the Press Branch. Quite a number of ice boats had survived but *Marbury* was one of the best examples of a Shropshire Union type then in existence.

In 1968 the Shropshire Union Canal Society needed a work boat and I negotiated the sale of *Marbury* from British Waterways for a nominal £20.00. We raised the boat and bow hauled her down the canal. She can now be seen as part of the historic boat collection at the National Waterways Museum, Ellesmere Port.

Perhaps one of the most outstanding acts of official vandalism was the breaking up of one of the last canal passenger packet boats *Duchess Countess* – despite published claims that she was to be preserved – which had survived in field by the canal at Frankton. Built for the fast carriage of passengers and goods on the Bridgewater Canal she had become the home of a Mr. Mackey (spellings vary) and much of her was very much in original condition, as these Eric de Maré photographs of the exterior and interior taken in 1948 illustrate. Parts were kept but subsequently destroyed in a fire and all that now remains are the distinctive S-shaped bow knife that these boats carried and a name board, in the National Waterways Museum, Stoke Bruerne. Fortunately, before *Duchess Countess* was destroyed, she was measured and drawn by marine architect and wooden boat expert David R. MacGregor, and The Duchess Countess Trust – based on the Montgomery Canal at Llanymynech – is planning to build a replica.

Over the years *Duchess Countess* owner Mackey has acquired the reputation of a recluse, but this wartime photograph of Welsh Frankton Home Guard shows that he joined in with local life. Mackey is fourth from the left in the back row.

Opposite the junction at Trevor are two dry docks which are the main surviving features of the canal company's boatyard. The Shropshire Union's main boatbuilding centre was at Tower Wharf in Chester but many boats were built here. In the 1920s the Trevor yard still employed up to six boatbuilders, a foreman, a blacksmith, a painter and other assistants. The boat on the uncovered dock is the *Symbol* which was one of a batch of six Shropshire Union fly-boats actually built here at Trevor whilst a strike was in progress at the Chester dock. At this time she was – with her sister vessel *Saturn* – one of two surviving boats of her type and was the subject of the first attempt by volunteers of the Shropshire Union Fly-boat Restoration Society to preserve such a vessel. Unfortunately, it was the days before major funding was available from grant giving bodies like the Heritage Lottery Fund and *Symbol's* condition deteriorated beyond repair. She had to be dismantled, but a number of key parts have however been preserved with other fly-boat artefacts. The Society were ultimately successful – in a partnership with British Waterways Wales & Border Counties – in obtaining and restoring *Saturn*.

Contrasting times at Wrenbury. The elaborately decorated cabin side of one of Arthur Sumner Limited's carrying boats, which operated from their Wrenbury Mill premises, seen on Chester dock.

Being linked to a structural engineering company, when English Country Cruises took over Wrenbury Mill they installed this ingenious combined dock and lift for servicing their hire boats. Sumners would have been impressed!

One of a series of somewhat revolutionary craft introduced by British Waterways in the 1950s were these weed cutting boats; the one allocated to this area being seen at Swanley. A few still survive and a particularly good example can be seen in the boat collection at the National Waterways Museum, Ellesmere Port.

Checking of boat licences has always been a bone of contention and in the late 1970s British Waterways introduced licence patrol inspectors and provided them with this *Ranger* class of boats. Based on those used on the Thames, their V-shaped hulls were totally unsuitable for narrow canals. Although apparently afloat, *Ranger* 1 is holed and sitting on the bottom here by Gledrid Bridge.

The *Sirius* is seen fresh from docking by the side of the Ellesmere dry dock and painted in the original British Waterways livery; so the date must be shortly after nationalisation. It is unusual in that it is an ex-Grand Union Canal Carrying Company boat and was seen regularly as a maintenance boat on the Shropshire Union system. The lady in the hatches is Mrs Littler. She and her husband – known as 'Nibby' – were the last to live on a maintenance boat (the *Sagitta*) on the Norbury section in the 1960s.

Until the advent of specially built motorised maintenance craft ex carrying company motor narrowboats were not popular among the men on this canal because of their deep draft; although a number from ex north west fleets were tried. Despite that, Alf Owen and his wife were making a fair speed with the *Weaver* after leaving Swanley Locks in October 1960.

Immaculately clean and rigged by Jack Roberts, the *Antwerp* is moored at Trefor to welcome aboard members of the Railway & Canal Historical Society for a visit to Pontcysyllte Aqueduct on 8 September 1956. Jack and his mate were also the means of propulsion as the boat was bow hauled across.

A local lad poses at the helm of the ex-Mersey Weaver company motor boat *Sheila* whilst Tom Godwin was taking her back to Northwich in the 1950s. Another boat that was found to be unsuitable for this canal, she probably finished up with many more of her ilk – sunk in the flashes on the Trent & Mersey Canal or an old lock cut on the River Weaver.

Boatbuilder Jack (John) Moody working in the yard at Ellesmere – in the top picture with Tom Godwin. Jack Moody lived next to the yard and was immortalised by Eric de Maré by being pictured in his seminal book *Canals of England*. More detail of the elaborate overhead transportation system can also be seen in these pictures.

In an obviously posed picture *Tramp* – now modified with a sort of clerestory roof – is moored at New Marton Bridge while Mrs Eaton Parker posts a letter. A note on the back of the print describes it as "a bargees letter box". Although appearing somewhat inaccessible, the New Marton lock keeper posted his daily returns from this remote box – but that was in the days when we had a real postal service!

An unidentified ex-fly boat being used on bank repair work near Frankton in October 1961. By the size of the concrete mixer, the boat's stability and health and safety were not major considerations then.

Possibly the last horse to work on maintenance on the Llangollen Canal? Eddie steers our boat carefully past boats loaded with clay near Bettisfield in October 1960, after BW men had told us to turn around as the canal had burst near Llangollen. British Waterways had no horses by then and this one was hired from a man who bred fine animals and with his wife ran Bettisfield Post Office; although the harness was supplied by BW. Recalling this occasion sometime later, when I was involved in running a horse-drawn passenger boat, I asked about the harness and someone at Ellesmere Yard (with a knowing smile) 'denied all knowledge' of it. So off I went to Bettisfield Post Office, found the harness – still immaculately kept – hanging in the stable and I gave the man £5.00 for it. A very satisfactory outcome for all concerned and I believe – although possibly much repaired – it is still in use today. The inset shows a brass from this harness – a lasting memory of horses working for the Shropshire Union Railway & Canal Company on the Llangollen Canal.

Boats with all the luxuries of a floating home, watched by visiting sun-shaded tourists, and housed in specially built marinas, with plug-in amenities, might generate a measure of spinning-in-the-grave reaction among past generations of Shropshire Union working boatmen; but they would have much appreciated the comforts! This is the modern face of the Llangollen Canal and if the leisure revolution ensures the survival of this waterway for at least another 200 years – so be it. But please take time to think of, learn about and appreciate this waterway's glorious working past.

Acknowledgements

Much of what I first learned about this waterway was told to me by boatman, Jack Roberts, who taught Eddie Frangleton and myself all about Shropshire Union history, boats and boating. Eddie is my oldest friend from schooldays and has boated on the Llangollen with us from our first trip. Sometimes we are not sure who took what photograph!

Much help also came from my friends, authors, artists and historians, Tony Lewery, Edward Paget-Tomlinson and Charles Hadfield. Special thanks to Tony for the cover artwork. Also from friends and acquaintances, past and present, in British Waterways, particularly Brian Haskins, R.H.J (Bob) Cotton, Tony Condor, Howard Griffiths, Jim Howard, Vanessa Wiggins, Sheila Doeg and all the Wales & Border Counties staff. Not forgetting all my friends involved with me in The Shropshire Union Fly-boat Restoration Society.

Thanks for the loan of historic photographs, illustrations and items of information and other help to – Tom Godwin – particularly for his collection of snapshots taken whilst working at Ellesmere Yard – the Roberts family, Graham Palmer, Roger Butler, Dennis Darlington, Dusty Miller, David Moore, Ian L.Wright, Owen Prosser, Geoff Taylor, Mrs Nora Beech, Mrs Joan Rush, H.R.D. Lindop, the National Railway Museum, Hugh Potter and *Waterways World* magazine, Dennis Hobson-Greenwood, the Hyde family, Martin Grundy, Paul Sillitoe, Joseph Boughey, Mike Webb, John Stothert, Alf Owen, Peter Brown, the Wade family, Eric de Maré, The Waterways Trust and for the map, Roy Davenport and *Canals & Rivers* magazine. All other photographs were taken by myself or are from my Waterway Images photographic library.

Thanks also to all the staff at Landmark Publishing.

Last, but by far from least, to my wife Beryl, daughter Julie and son Mike and his family, for all their contributions, loving help and encouragement.

The majority of the photographs in this book are from the Waterway Images Photographic Library, specialising in all facets of rivers and canals: their history, traditions, craft, architecture and environment – past and present. For details, telephone 01283 790447 or 01538 361138 or visit the website at www.waterwayimages.com

---

Further Information on the Llangollen Canal

The navigation authority for the Llangollen Canal is –
British Waterways Wales & Border Counties Waterways
www.waterscape.com or *walesandbordercounties@britishwaterways.co.uk*

There are also a number of voluntary groups involved with the waterway -

The Inland Waterways Association, Shrewsbury District & North Wales Branch
shrewsandwales@waterways.org.uk

The Shropshire Union Canal Society
www.shropshireunion.org.uk

The Whitchurch Waterways Trust
www.wwtrust.org.uk

The Shropshire Union Fly-boat Restoration Society
www.saturnflyboat.org.uk